Handwriting Analysis

Vijaya Kumar

NEW DAWN PRESS, INC.
USA• UK• INDIA

NEW DAWN PRESS GROUP

Published by New Dawn Press Group
New Dawn Press, Inc., 244 South Randall Rd # 90, Elgin, IL 60123
e-mail: sales@newdawnpress.com

New Dawn Press, 2 Tintern Close, Slough, Berkshire, SL1-2TB, UK
e-mail: ndpuk@newdawnpress.com

New Dawn Press (An Imprint of Sterling Publishers (P) Ltd.)
A-59, Okhla Industrial Area, Phase-II, New Delhi-110020
e-mail: info@sterlingpublishers.com
www.sterlingpublishers.com

Handwriting Analysis
©2005, Sterling Publishers Pvt. Ltd., New Delhi
ISBN 1 84557 123 1

Reprint 2007

PRINTED IN INDIA

Contents

Preface

This book is by no means an extensive study by any professional. The data provided in this book are my own interpretations of the subject, gleaned from various books, and presented from a layperson's viewpoint.
The book deals with each aspect of the study, point by point, in a simple language and serves as a ready reckoner for those who have no time to go through heavy in-depth studies.

The publishers and I hold no responsibility for any discrepancy in the script. We would welcome suggestions or intimation of errors that come to anybody's notice.

Vijaya Kumar

Introduction

Graphology is a scientific study and analysis of handwriting, especially of a person's personality. It may open windows to numerous unexplored areas for anyone interested in practising this skill. It is an exciting and beneficial key to unlocking the potential within you.

Handwriting must be studied, taking into consideration the formation of letters and words, the spacing between letters, words and lines. Since some people write differently at different times, their analysis also differs at these times. And no two handwritings are identical. As a self-awareness and an improvement tool, graphology is probably the fastest way one can learn about another's personality and behaviour with great accuracy.

Slant Factors

- *A slant denotes the writer's emotional direction and degree of emotional control.*
- *Generally, a right-slanted writer leans towards the future, friendships, compliance and extroversion, while a left-slanted one leans back to the past and away from people, towards introversion and self, having more time and energy for creative pursuits.*

Moderate Right Slant

1. Communicative and zestful
2. Extrovert and gregarious
3. Warm, affectionate and amicable
4. Sensitive, compassionate and sympathetic
5. Future orientation
6. Somewhat impulsive
7. Expressive
8. Courageous

for the last few
years, they have
been lying low.
No matter what,
they have stuck

Extreme Right Slant

1. Extremely insecure and dependent on others
2. Very impulsive
3. Unrestrained and bombastic, capable of hysteria
4. Very passionate
5. Suspicious
6. Very expressive
7. Sensitive
8. Possessive
9. Intense

The Chinese invented printing about a thousand years ago, using characters made of porcelain.

Moderate Left Slant

1. Reflective, withdrawn and independent
2. Non-sympathetic, non-compassionate, unaffectionate, insensitive and unfriendly
3. Shy, introvert and non-communicative
4. Depressed, fearful and anxious
5. Choosy about materials and things concerning self

Vast numbers of liny.
plants and animals
float and drift in
the sea. Many of

Extreme Left Slant

1. Repressed childhood
2. Insecure and fearful of life itself
3. Emotionally withdrawn
4. Evades reality
5. Apprehensive of intimacy
6. Defensive

It measures the angle of the sun's or a star's altitude above the horizon

Vertical Slant

1. Ambivalent
2. Self-controlled
3. Independent
4. Self-restrained
5. Head controls the heart
6. Matter-of-fact personality
7. Self-reliant

When you are asleep,
the electrical activity
in the brain is quite
different from when you

Irregular Slant

1. Extremely sensitive
2. Moody and thoughtful
3. Unpredictable and erratic behaviour
4. Versatile
5. Ambivalent
6. Nervous and excitable

He does not walk on two feet, but on all four like the animals around

Size of Script

- *The size of a script projects our self-esteem and self-importance.*
- *It depicts the smallness or largeness of our thoughts and life experience.*

Small Size of Script
1. Meticulous and observant
2. Modest, reserved and restrained
3. Mentally alert, resourceful and thrifty
4. Lacks self-confidence

Convenient medicines are those which can be taken or administered easily by the patient himself. Oral medicine

Large Size of Script

1. Bold and aggressive
2. Ambitious for name, fame and recognition
3. Enthusiastic, confident and optimistic
4. Boastful and extrovert
5. Lacks concentration and discipline
6. Strongly motivated

The small, or
even the large,
sweet which some
people suck in

Moderate Size of Script

1. Conservative, conventional and traditional
2. Practical and realistic
3. Moderate in thinking and attitude
4. Honest
5. Adaptable
6. Sincere

A rainbow appears
in the sky when
there is rain while
the sun is shining.

Tall Size of Script
1. Ambitious
2. Far-sighted
3. Lack of modesty, consideration, tact and objectivity
4. Observant

The world's highest
mountain is Mount
Everest, on the

Broad Size of Script

1. Boastful, egoistic and proud
2. Frank, friendly and sociable
3. Imaginative, spontaneous and artistic
4. Indiscreet, and lacks discipline and tact
5. Self-assured

Mercator's new
projection thus
increased the

Narrow Size of Script

1. Conservative
2. Distrustful and suspicious
3. Economic
4. Self-controlled and moderate
5. Shy and passive
6. Inhibited
7. Introvert
8. Selective and critical

This was originally the padded coat worn beneath a breastplate. Later it became the main garment

Variable Size of Script

1. Moody and short-tempered
2. Self-centered
3. Indecisive and inconsistent
4. Naive and immature
5. Excitable and unpredictable
6. Emotionally off-balance

> *The Titanic was the largest and most luxurious liner of her time when she set out on her*

Spacing

- *Letter Spacing – shows the extent to which a writer relies upon cooperation with others.*

Close Letter Spacing
1. Repressed
2. Scared
3. Selfish
4. Hostile
5. Inhibited
6. Resentful

The Italian government has now embarked on the difficult project of trying to keep this marvel of medieval and renaissance architecture and engineering

Wide Letter Spacing

1. Extrovert
2. Sympathetic
3. Spendthrift
4. Considerate

Clouds vary in shape
according to their
height and tempera-
ture, and they contain

- *Word Spacing – shows the degree of contact the writer establishes with his or her immediate environment.*

Even Word Spacing
1. Reasonable and well-balanced
2. Self-confident and amiable

Astronomers have
found out a lot
about the stars.
They know that

Uneven Word Spacing

1. Insecure
2. Spontaneous
3. Changeable social attitude
4. Gullible

Fault-mountains are formed when the earth's crust cracks, or faults,

Variable Word Spacing

1. Moody and emotionally off-balance
2. Self-centered and short-tempered
3. Indecisive, immature and naive
4. Excitable and unpredictable

How do stars form? Dust and gas in the rebula come together.

Close Word Spacing

1. Self-centered
2. Needs to interact with others
3. Seeks attention
4. Talkative
5. Insecure
6. Spontaneous and impulsive
7. Introvert

Rainwater and melted snow collect in hollows in high grounds such as mountains and hills. The water then flows down by the steepest route. The steeper the slope, the faster the river

Wide Word Spacing

1. Inhibited, shy and an isolationist
2. Introvert
3. Critical
4. Philosophical
5. Cultured
6. Opinionated
7. Self-conscious

> The dugong is a gentle, harmless sea mammal which basks in the shallow waters of the Pacific

- *Line Spacing – a reflection of the writer's direction, concern for order and valuation of time.*

Even Line Spacing
1. Well-balanced
2. Harmonious
3. Flexible

> Vast numbers of tiny plants
> and animals float and drift
> in the sea. Many of them
> are so small that they can
> be seen only under a

Wide Line Spacing

1. Objective
2. Fearful of contact and closeness
3. Suspicious and hostile
4. Mentally agile
5. Not spontaneous
6. Well-mannered

To skiyak, you need two narrow, elongated boats

Narrow Line Spacing

1. Thrifty and frugal
2. Fear of isolation and distance
3. Lack of reserve
4. Forceful
5. Creative

Mendel studied plants,
especially the garden pea,
and showed that, the
inherited characteristics
were the result of

Zones

1. The upper zone determines intellect, imagination, spiritualism, intensity, conscience, ambition, creativity and fantasy, the middle zone for daily action, social work, and matters of immediate concern, and the lower for desires and drives.

Upper Zone

Middle Zone

Lower Zone

2. The letters *b, d, h, k,* and *t* in lower case use the middle and upper zones.

she drove like a big killer. They looked at her in

3. The letters *g, j, p, y* and *z* in lower case occupy the middle and lower zones.

giggling and gurgling jalopy just for joy privately pay premium

4. The letter *f* is tri-zonal, and the only lower case letter to use all the three zones.

from far fields further

5. All capital letters use the upper and middle zones, while *g, y* and *z* are tri-zonal depending upon each one's style of using capital letters.

Paris Madras Chicago

Grand Yearly Zests

Upper Zone

1. An inflated upper zone reveals one's imagination, spiritualism, intellect and thought.

2. The more flourished or enlarged or twirled, the more extreme is the imagination.

3. A compressed upper zone depicts one's lack of self-image, creativity or imagination, or goals.

4. A narrow, high upper zone indicates cautious thoughts with interest in abstract matters.

1. middleman's land
   his hand held

2. middleman's land
   his hand held

3. middleman's land
   his hand held

4. middleman's land
   his hand held

Middle Zone

1. An inflated middle zone shows immaturity, conceit, a tendency to exaggerate, boredom and a confined sense of feeling.

2. A compressed middle zone shows lack of interest in everyday social and work life.

1. Later studies
   have shown
   that the genes
   are carried

2. Later studies
   have shown
   that the genes
   are carried

Lower Zone

1. An inflated lower zone shows one's need for money willfulness, sexual drives that need to be satisfied, and wastage of time and money.

2. An angular lower loop indicates hostility, uncompromising resentment, and difficulty in sexual gratification.

3. No loop whatsoever suggests materialistic and sexual repression.

4. Very short lower loops indicate that the person is lethargic, and attaches no importance to basic drives or materialism.

1. people's lungs are paralysed

2. go for a fiery and fast days

3. giving off the bright light we need

4. Mary's everyday graduated scale

Pressure

- *Pressure is the graphologist's measure of the writer's determination, intensity and vitality, and shows the force or lack of it in the person's personality.*

Heavy Pressure

1. Aggressive, possessive, short-tempered, abusive, violent domineering and egoistic
2. Creative, enthusiastic, sensuous, and enduring
3. Emotionally strong and deeply committed
4. A go-getter who is successful

Agriculture was practised on a larger scale. Simple

Light Pressure

1. Sensitive, tender, forgiving, adaptable, tolerant and spiritual
2. Passively indifferent, weak-willed, non-committal and lacks vitality
3. Physically weak and fragile
4. Prefers pastel colours

The best known of these pigs is the white Yorkshire pig,

Medium Pressure

1. Moderately energetic
2. Cooperative
3. Sociable
4. Calm and collected
5. Shuns extremes and is balanced

When snow comes into contact with salt it does not

General Types

- *There are four kinds of connecting strokes – garland, arcade, angular and threaded.*
- *The garland, a rounded and cuplike stroke, suggests receptivity, and openness to all influences.*
- *The arcade, an arched stroke, shows the person to be artistic and one seeking protection.*
- *The angular stroke suggests irresolution or discomfort.*
- *The threaded stroke reveals a person who dislikes being categorised, and has an intuitive capacity for attaining temporary identification.*

Garland Stroke

A deep garland shows one to be depressive, indifferent, gullible, insecure, passive, contemplative and lacking restraint.

A shallow garland suggests one to be reckless, unrestrained, superficial, amiable and well mannered.

A moderate one shows one to be charming, gracious, flexible, kind, extrovert, diplomatic, careless and lazy.

Machines provide
more power to
do work with,

Arcade Stroke

A moderate arcade shows one to be creative, artistic, meditative, gentle, protective, poised, shy, formal, proud and authoritative.

A flat one means the person is scheming, secretive, pretentious, gullible, eccentric and defensive.

> created for man's
> welfare. Others
> were used as

Angular Stroke

A moderate angle shows one to be analytical, shrewd, logical, competitive, firm, steadfast, success-oriented, ambitious, energetic, determined, excitable, disciplined, persistent and idealistic.

A flat one suggests that the person is aggressive, cold-blooded, intolerant, dissatisfied, stubborn, self-centered, critical, forceful, slow and thorough.

> *must still eat*
> *a good deal of*
> *meat, or other*

Threaded Stroke

A well-threaded stroke shows versatility, perception, intuition, intelligence, independence, seeking appreciation rather than reward.

A badly threaded stroke means one is indecisive, unpredictable, insecure, nervous, impatient, fearful, cunning, perceptive, insightful and crafty.

Control of body
temperature is exercised
by a centre in the

Individual Letters

- *The conventional forms of the letters indicate a conventional and orthodox behaviour.*
- *The flourished, ornamental or decorative form depicts a creative and artistic flair.*
- *Weird and unusual forms reveal an eccentric and weird behaviour.*

Capital Letters

1. Capital letters denote the image that the writer likes to project.
2. The greater the size of the capital, the greater the pride, the confidence, and the vanity of the writer.
3. Ornamental capitals represent ostentation and self-consciousness.
4. Printed capitals show that one is constructive.

Capital Letter 'I'

Inflated

1. Egoistic, proud and vain
2. Creative, imaginative and impressive

Deflated

1. Timid and repressed

Left-tilting

1. Introvert, cautious and suspicious
2. Insecure and defensive

Right-tilting
1. Extrovert
2. Needs attention, praise, affection and approval

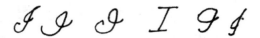

Vertical
1. Independent and unemotional
2. Loves privacy

Printed 'I'
1. Straightforward
2. Intelligent and versatile
3. Simple and modest

Small Letter 'i'

Dot High above Stem

1. Imaginative and a dreamer
2. Spiritually inclined

spiritual , timid,

Dot at Right of Stem

1. Fast thinker
2. Impulsive and impatient

did the right thing

Dot at Left of Stem

1. Timid and cautious
2. Procrastinates
3. Lacks confidence

did the right thing

Wavy Dot

1. Good sense of humour
2. Fun-loving

did the right thing

Circled Dot

1. Loyal
2. Faddish and needs attention
3. Imaginative and artistic

It lives in its

Absence of Dot

1. Absent-minded, with poor memory
2. Careless

it lives in its

Flying 'V' Dot

1. Sarcastic, cruel and irritable
2. Domineering

it lives in its

Tented Dot

1. Critical and brutal
2. Short-tempered

it lives in its

Letter 't'

Average Balanced Bar Crossing

1. Balanced and organised
2. Self-controlled, calm and firm
3. Precise

that the thoughts took up the time

Cross to Left

1. Procrastinates
2. Indecisive
3. Lives in the past

that the thoughts took up the time

Cross to Right

1. Impulsive and tactless
2. Enthusiastic and energetic
3. Rebellious and irritable
4. A fast thinker

that the thoughts took up the time

Down-Slanted
1. Destructive, brutal and cruel
2. Argumentative and aggressive
3. Determined
4. Despondent

the truth of the matter is that

Up-Slanted
1. Optimistic and aggressive
2. Enthusiastic and ambitious

the truth of the matter is that

Bar above Stem
1. Imaginative and daydreamer
2. Unrealistic goals and spiritual

The Truth of The matter is That

Low Bar on the Stem
1. Inferiority complex
2. Low goals
3. Patient and humble
4. Self-doubter

the terrible thoughts
that tell you the

Short Bar
1. Underachiever
2. Lacks drive and willpower

the terrible thoughts
that tell you that

Long Bar
1. Enthusiastic and ambitious
2. Bold and energetic
3. Confident and bossy

the terrible thoughts
that tell you that

Absent Bar

1. Absent-minded
2. Careless and inattentive to details
3. Hasty and rebellious

lake notice of liny

Wavy Bar

1. Humorous and good-natured
2. Intuitive
3. Frivolous and wishy-washy

take notice of tiny

Starlike 't'

1. Sense of responsibility
2. Stubborn and sensitive

take notice of tiny

Tented

1. Defensive and cautious

take notice of tiny

Crossing Back

1. Introvert, egoistic and jealous
2. Possible withdrawal to past
3. Lacks confidence and insecure

together at the turn

Down-Turned Hook

1. Bitter and greedy
2. Revengeful

Together at the turn

Upturned Hook

1. Stubborn
2. Tenacious

together at the turn

Looped Stem

1. Sensitive
2. Articulate
3. Bothered by criticism

together at the turn

Letter 'a' and 'o'

Double-looped

1. Dishonest to self and others
2. Insincere, shy and crafty

an onion and a

Open at Top

1. Talkative, open-minded, can't keep a secret
2. Honest, sincere and generous
3. Reticent and cautious

an onion and a

Open at Bottom

1. Dishonest and an embezzler

an onion and a

Closed and clean

1. Honest, reserved and secretive

and onion and a

Letter 'b'

Bottom Portion Open

1. Gullible and trusting

but buttresses better

Bottom Portion Closed

1. Cautious and business minded
2. Suspicious and secretive

But Buttresses Better

Tall and Narrow

1. Idealistic or religious
2. Unexpressive

but buttresses better

Short and Full

1. Humble and self-loving

but buttresses better

Without Upper Loop

1. Intelligent and tasteful

but buttresses better

Letter 'c'

Crowns or Loops

1. Vain and pretentious
2. Rigid
3. May be artistic

creative creatures
call crafted cases

Beginning Stroke

1. Ambitious

creative creatures
call crafted cases

Plain

1. Idealistic
2. Simple and gracious

creative creatures
call crafted cases

Letter 'd'

Loopy Stem
  1. Sensitive and imaginative

drop dead and

Tall and Unlooped Stem
  1. Idealistic and independent
  2. Dignified and proud

drop dead and

Short and Unlooped Stem
  1. Modest and humble
  2. Cautious and reduced concentration

drop dead and

Tall and Wide Loop
  1. Very sensitive
  2. Vain, arrogant and conceited

drop dead and

Bottom Open

1. Unreliable
2. Dishonest

clark cleeds that
defy clealing and

Body Closed

1. Secretive about affairs

dark deeds that
defy dealing and

Left Flag

1. Protective, musical, creative

dark deeds that
defy dealing and

Letter 'e'

Closed Loop

1. Critical and skeptical
2. Quick thinker
3. Suspicious and secretive

earmarked ends

Broad Loop

1. Broad-minded
2. Talkative and outspoken

earmarked ends

Greek 'e'

1. Cultured and aesthetic

earmarked ends

Narrow Loop

1. Critical
2. Narrow-minded

earmarked ends

Letter 'f'

Balanced Upper and Lower Parts
1. Well-organised and planned
2. Balanced and poised

fearfully fleshy

Absent Upper Loop
1. Self-opinionated
2. Practical

fearfully fleshy

Large Lower Loop
1. Active and energetic

fearfully fleshy

Large Upper Loop
1. Articulate

fearfully fleshy

Angular Form
1. Resentful and stubborn
2. Opinionated
3. Uncompromising

for fear of falling
off the first free

Fluid Form
1. Altruistic and original
2. Fluid or smooth thinker
3. Pleasure-loving

for fear of falling
off the first free

Cross Form
1. High concentration
2. Fatalism

for fear of falling
off the first free

Letters 'g', 'q', 'y' and 'z'

Long Stem

1. Narrow-minded

great hazy quay

Rounded Full Loop

1. Gregarious and loyal
2. Interested in saving money

great hazy quay

Absent Loop

1. Practical and aggressive

great hazy quay

Triangular Stem

1. Opinionated and critical
2. Tenacious, compulsive and aggressive

great hazy quay

Resembling Number '8'

1. Intellectual, altruistic and adaptable
2. Understanding

great haggler giggles

Letter 'h', 'k' and 'l'

Short Loop

1. Lazy, indifferent and immature
2. Materialistic, lacking spiritual values

hooked handles

Tall and Narrow Loop

1. Spiritual
2. Rigid and reserved

hooked handles

Tall and Wide Loop

1. Spiritually aware
2. Seeks greater social interests

hooked handles

Absent Loop

1. Practical and intelligent
2. Blunt and outspoken

hooked handles

Letters 'm' and 'n'

Rounded

1. Slow, lazy and immature
2. Cautious, gentle and analytical

more often than

Peaked

1. A bright thinker with a sharp mind

more often than

Initial Stroke Large and Flourishing

1. Diplomatic, executive ability

more often than

Final Stroke Higher than Others

1. Eccentric and stubborn

more often than

Graceful First Stroke

1. Good-natured and amiable

more often than

Letter 'p'

Large Loop

1. Physically active
2. Likes sports and dances

physically poor

Short Upper Stem

1. Expects rewards
2. Unwilling to go out of the way

physically poor

High Upper Stem

1. Charitable
2. Toils without expectations

physically poor

Open Body

1. Talkative
2. Spendthrift

physically poor

Letter 'r'

Flat Topped

1. Broadminded
2. Planning ability
3. Skilful with tools

roar really

Double Peaked

1. Finger dexterity
2. Perceptive and clever

roar really

Initial Stroke Looped

1. Proud and stubborn

roar really

Parochial 'r'

1. Artistic and musical
2. Suppressed thinking

roar really

Letter 's'

Printed 's'
1. Artistic
2. Cultured

some say she

Upper Peak
1. Stubborn
2. Curious and investigative

some say she

Rounded Top
1. Yielding
2. Pushover

some say she

Enrolled
1. Shrewd
2. Greedy

some say she

Loops

1. The height and width of a loop depicts one's mental interests and spiritualism, and one's social and gregarious nature, respectively.

2. Loops in moderation indicate mental stability and well-being.

3. Exaggerated loops suggest that the person is an extrovert, sympathetic, social, intuitive, impulsive and compassionate.

4. Scanty and narrow loops denote repressed emotional feelings.

he feels his face crinkling, making him look crinkled

Knots, Hooks and Claws

1. Knotted letters depict a person who is tenacious, persistent and logical.
2. The upward turning claws and hooks show a person to be materialistic, greedy, vindictive, and cannot stand opposition.
3. The downward turning claws and hooks show a person to be forceful and bitter, apart from having all the traits that the upturned claws and hooks show.

Signatures

- *A signature is the image that one likes to project to the outer world.*
- *A signature is not necessarily the way one is, especially when its style differs from the main body of the writing.*

Smaller than Script

1. Introvert and shy
2. Unpretentious
3. Oversensitive and insecure
4. Calm and mild
5. Humble
6. Submissive

light fades
and we
see the

Ruchith Shrivastava

Larger than Script

1. Extrovert, ambitious and proud
2. Confident and secure
3. Wants recognition

us like a ton of bricks !

Corinna Corpus

Left Slanting with Script Right-Slanting

1. Pretentious
2. Projects a descriptive image

Right Slanting with Script Left-Slanting or Vertical

1. Pretends to be an extrovert
2. A private person

of hard skin, often
painful, which can

Vertical with Script Vertical or Left-Slanting

1. Appears in control to the world
2. Balanced and down to earth
3. Self-confident

photo receptors. The
effect is much similar

Sandhya Rani

Illegible with Legible Writing

1. A good communicator but likes to be incognito
2. Could be secretive, insecure and impatient
3. Hostile and inconsiderate
4. Egoistic

separate fields
of vision overlap

Illegible with Illegible Writing

1. Unconcerned
2. Dishonest
3. Egocentric
4. Impatient

Encircled

1. Desire for privacy
2. Excessively secretive
3. Self-interested

Crossed-Out Signature

1. Self-destructive
2. Hostility towards self

Margins

- *Margins show the writer's degree of economy, consistency, tolerance, desire for esteem, and urge for acceptance.*
- *Well-spaced margins denote an intelligent arrangement of time and space accompanied by favourable organisation.*

Wide Upper Margin

1. Modest and formal
2. Reserved and withdrawn

Experience tells us that the farther away an object is, the smaller it looks. Its colour also

Wide Lower Margin

1. Idealistic
2. Superficial
3. Aloof and reserved

> *Stereoscopic vision, or vision in depth, which we share with apes and monkeys. Most*

Wide Left Margin

1. Self-respect and high standards
2. Avoids the past and has courage in facing life
3. Shy and keeps distance from others
4. Late riser

> *To them the world appears flat One exerts too much pressure and all that*

Wide Right Margin

1. Reserved and fearful of future
2. Oversensitive, self-conscious and fastidious
3. Extravagant and wasteful
4. Unrealistic and unsocial

> The change in
> the position of the
> eyes from the
> side of the head

Narrow Upper Margin

1. Informal
2. Direct
3. Lacks respect
4. Indifferent

> ~~thirst~~ . is caused by
> the body's need for
> water. The mouth
> feels dry, and
> drinking is a but

Narrow Lower Margin

1. Sentimental and sensuous
2. Materialistic
3. Depressed
4. Communicative
5. Fatigued

> we smile to show
> our pleasures or
> amusements in
> something or with

Narrow Left Margin

1. Shy and unsociable
2. Depressed
3. Lacks spontaneity
4. Tendency to fall ill

> From all directions
> ripples of sound come
> to our ears. Sound
> travels through the

Narrow Right Margin

1. Loves travelling
2. Unwise thriftiness
3. Ambivalent social attitude

> By the time the
> baby is eighteen to
> twenty months old,
> the fontanelle has
> naturally closed, and

Uneven Margin at Left

1. Rebellious and defiant
2. Unbalanced and disorganized
3. Versatile
4. Tolerant

> At the top end
> it is attached to
> your scapula, or
> shoulder blade.

Uneven Margin at Right

1. Impulsive
2. Unreliable reactions
3. Unwisely thrifty

The advanced forms
of textile production
of long threads

Absence of Margins

1. Insecure and fearful of death
2. Frugal and stingy
3. Tactless, talkative and gullible
4. Kind and hospitable
5. Fond of luxury and acquisition
6. Morbidly curious

> Nowadays, many larger farms tend to attack such wild animals, and

Connected and Disconnected Writing

- *Connected writing shows the attitude of the writer towards others.*
- *Disconnected writing is a gesture of isolation, of enclosure, and it may lead to attractive new wholes or to withdrawal.*

Connected

Good: Analytical, logical and objective, calculating, organized, rational, practical and realistic

Bad: Restless, inconsiderate, tactless and compulsive

connected

The state of Israel was established in nineteen forty-eight.

Disconnected

Good: Perceptive, intuitive, imaginative, observant, inventive and sensitive

Bad: Aloof, lonely, insecure, moody, selfish, suspicious, shy, restless, inconsistent, illogical and impractical

<u>disconnected</u>

The state of Israel was established in nineteen forty-eight.